# SmOG, OIL SPILLS, SewAGE, AND MoRE

## THE YUCKY POLLUTION BOOK

Alvin and Virginia Silverstein
and Laura Silverstein Nunn

Illustrated by
Gerald Kelley

**Library of Congress Cataloging-in-Publication Data:**

Silverstein, Alvin.
    Smog, oil spills, sewage, and more : the yucky pollution book / by Dr. Alvin Silverstein,
Virginia Silverstein, and Laura Silverstein Nunn.
        p. cm. — (Yucky science)
    Includes bibliographical references and index.
    Summary: "Gives an overview of different types of pollution, with interesting scientific
and historical facts"—Provided by publisher.
    ISBN 978-0-7660-3313-9
    1. Pollution—Juvenile literature. 2. Environmental protection—Juvenile literature.
I. Silverstein, Virginia B. II. Nunn, Laura Silverstein. III. Title.
    TD176.S54 2011
    363.73—dc22
                                            2009021274

Printed in the United States of America

052010 Lake Book Manufacturing, Inc., Melrose Park, IL

10 9 8 7 6 5 4 3 2 1

**To Our Readers:** We have done our best to make sure all Internet Addresses in this book
were active and appropriate when we went to press. However, the author and the publisher
have no control over and assume no liability for the material available on those Internet sites
or on other Web sites they may link to. Any comments or suggestions can be sent by e-mail to
comments@enslow.com or to the address on the back cover.

♻ Enslow Publishers, Inc., is committed to printing our books on recycled paper. The paper
in every book contains 10% to 30% post-consumer waste (PCW). The cover board on the
outside of each book contains 100% PCW. Our goal is to do our part to help young people
and the environment too!

**Illustration Credits:** © 2009 Gerald Kelley, www.geraldkelley.com

**Photo Credits:** Associated Press, pp. 12, 15, 17; CDC/ Dr. Edwin P. Ewing, Jr., p. 34 (top);
© Daniel Stein/iStockphoto.com, p. 8; Dr. John D. Cunningham/Visuals Unlimited, Inc.,
p. 11; © pmphoto/iStockphoto.com, p. 34 (bottom); Shutterstock, pp. 25, 30, 40, 42; © Zsolt
Biczó/iStockphoto.com, p. 29.

**Cover Illustration:** © 2009 Gerald Kelley, www.geraldkelley.com

**Enslow Publishers, Inc.**
40 Industrial Road
Box 398
Berkeley Heights, NJ 07922
USA
            http://www.enslow.com

# CONTENTS

# That's Yucky!

A few centuries ago, a walk down the street could be quite an adventure. People had to "watch their step" quite literally, if they wanted to avoid piles of dog poop and blobs of spit or vomit. Walkers had to watch their heads, too, when passing a house. At any moment an upstairs window might open so someone could throw out the "slops"—dirty dishwater, or perhaps a pot full of last night's pee and poop. All that yucky stuff was swept or washed by rain into the streets, where it flowed like a stinky river.

Meanwhile, backyards and empty lots were often used as handy places to dump garbage. Food wastes and leftovers, broken dishes and chairs—things people no longer wanted or needed—piled up there. Rats and mice scurried through those smelly piles in search of food.

These days we have better ways of taking care of those yucky throwaways. Flush toilets and underground sewers carry our body wastes and dirty dishwater to treatment centers. The water is cleaned before it is dumped into lakes, streams, or rivers. Regular trash collections take unwanted items to be buried, burned, or recycled into usable materials. But plenty of yucky things still wind up where they shouldn't be. Then they form pollution—substances that make air, soil, or water dirty or harmful to living things. From smoke and exhaust gases to oil spills, garbage dumps, and chemicals in our homes, the pollution in our air, water, roads, and fields can be disgusting and sometimes dangerous.

In this book we'll look at some of the yucky kinds of pollution in our world.

# Dirty Air

## HAZY SKIES

On a warm summer day, you will see it in any big city. A cloud of thick haze floats in the air among the tall buildings. Looking up at the sky, you might think that the dark hazy cloud was a sign of rain. But this is no rain cloud. It is a type of air pollution known as smog.

The term *smog* is actually a combination of two words: *smoke* and *fog*. Fog is a cloud that is close to the ground. It is a mix of air and tiny water droplets. The water droplets block out light, which makes it hard to see things through the fog. Smoke is the stuff that rises into the air from a burning fire. Tiny particles of soot and ash give it a dirty gray or brown color. Smoke also

**Los Angeles, California, is one of the smoggiest cities in the United States.**

includes gases. When a lot of smoke mixes with fog, it makes the air yucky.

Smog can get really thick sometimes. Then it not only looks dirty, it makes the air heavy and hard to breathe. It almost seems like you are breathing soup. In fact, in London people call bad smog a "peasouper."

Smog can make your eyes itchy, make you cough, and give you a runny nose and a sore throat. For people who have asthma or other lung problems, smog can make their condition much worse.

**Yikes!** If you blow your nose after a long day of breathing smog, the snot in the tissue may look gray or even black.

# CITY SMOKE

In the city, bumper-to-bumper traffic is just a part of everyday life. But crowded roads and highways mean lots and lots of pollution. Sitting in traffic, you may see trails of smoke coming from the exhaust pipes of cars, trucks, and buses. Sometimes you might even get a whiff—yuck! It smells so bad, you probably want to hold your nose. Cars also give off some poisonous gases that don't have any odor at all. One of these gases is carbon monoxide. You may not notice this gas, but large amounts can make it hard to breathe. Every day, cars and other vehicles pour enormous amounts of harmful chemicals into the air.

# Watch Out for Acid Rain!

Smog-filled skies contain lots of chemicals. When it rains, the raindrops pick up some of these chemicals. Then the raindrops become slightly acidic. This "acid rain" can have harmful effects on the environment. When it falls into lakes, rivers, and streams, it can kill fish and other water animals. Plant leaves turn brown and wrinkled. Some plants die. Acid rain also eats away at the surfaces of buildings, bridges, and statues.

**Acid rain damaged this statue.**

Factories also contribute to air pollution in a city. A factory's tall smokestacks send tons of black sooty smoke into the city air. It dirties not only the sky, but nearby buildings as well. Power plant smokestacks send out pollutants that include nitrogen oxide gas.

The soot and ash from the eruption of Mount Pinatubo in 1991 affected weather conditions for years afterward.

Nitrogen oxide plays a big role in forming smog. It can cause or worsen lung problems.

# IT'S RAINING FIRE!

People aren't always to blame for air pollution. Erupting volcanoes can shoot enormous amounts of yucky stuff into the air. An explosive eruption blasts gases, volcanic ash, lava, and hot pieces of rock into the air with tremendous force. The gases that spew out of a volcano include some very stinky chemicals that smell like rotten eggs.

Winds can carry the volcano's fiery insides through the air to other parts of the world. In fact, a powerful volcanic eruption can actually affect weather conditions all over the world. That happened in June 1991, for example, when Mount Pinatubo, a volcano in the Philippines, erupted. The soot, ash, and other substances thrown up into Earth's atmosphere blocked the Sun's rays. For two years the weather was cooler than usual all over the world.

# Icky Water

## DISASTER IN THE WATER

In March 1989, the *Exxon Valdez*, a big oil tanker, created a horrible mess off the coast of Alaska. It was carrying more than 53 million gallons of oil pumped out of nearby oil wells. The tanker smashed into a rocky reef and broke open, spilling out nearly 11 million gallons of oil into the Alaskan waters.

When the greasy, black oil hit the water, it spread out over the surface. The oil formed gooey clumps that stuck to everything they touched. Some of the oil washed onto shore, spreading thick patches of gummy black tar over sandy

Oil swirls out of the *Exxon Valdez* (top). The oil tanker spilled out nearly
11 million gallons of oil. It caused a lot of damage to nearby wildlife.

beaches and rocks. Spilled oil also sank to the sea bottom, killing the plants and animals living there.

The oil spill caused enormous damage to wildlife in the area. Greasy oil coated the feathers of waterbirds and the fur of seals and otters. It didn't just look and feel yucky—this pollution was deadly. Fluffy feathers and fur normally trap air that helps keep animals warm. But the oil made their coats stick closely to their bodies. Without the blanket of trapped air, many animals froze to death. The birds tried to clean their feathers, and the seals and otters licked their coats. But the oil they swallowed contained poisons. Hundreds of thousands of seabirds died, along with many

**Yikes!** The *Exxon Valdez* accident was the largest oil spill in U.S. history—that is, until April 20, 2010. On that date, the *Deepwater Horizon* oil-drilling rig exploded in the Gulf of Mexico. The rig had been drilling 5,000 miles (1,500 meters) below the surface of the sea. When it exploded, it created an oil gusher, with crude oil pouring into the seawater at up to 2.5 million gallons a day! After just a few months, the amount of oil polluting the area was close to 100 million gallons.

**It takes a lot of time, money, and effort to clean up after an oil spill.**

otters, harbor seals, and killer whales. The oil also poisoned fish eggs in the water.

Oil spills still happen, even deep in the sea. The explosion of a drilling rig in the Gulf of Mexico in April 2010 started an oil gusher on the ocean floor. It will take a lot of time and money to clean up the damage from this oil spill disaster.

# DOWN THE DRAIN

What happens to your pee and poop when you flush the toilet? Water washes it down through pipes that carry it out of the building. If you live in a rural area, your body wastes may go into a septic tank. This is a big tank underground. All that yucky stuff—the waste matter and wastewater that drains into the septic tank—is called sewage.

As wastewater enters the septic tank, the poop and other solids sink to the bottom, forming sludge. A layer of scum floats to the top. Bacteria, which are microscopic organisms, break down the gunk in the tank. (Bacteria make very stinky gases when they feed on sewage. That's why sewage smells so bad!) Eventually, water leaks out into the soil. Drain pipes help to filter out the yucky stuff. Finally the cleaned water flows down to the nearest underground stream. (And that is the water that you and your neighbors drink!)

In most cities and towns, the pipes from your kitchen and bathroom lead down to a sewer system. The sewer system runs underground. Sewer workers can get to the sewer by climbing down manholes that are scattered along the roads. Down in the sewer, water flows along like a river. But this "river" is filled with icky sewage and it smells really bad.

The sewer carries the city's wastewater to a sewage treatment plant, where it is cleaned. The treated water then flows out into a river or into the ocean. Eventually, this water becomes your drinking water. Normally, the water that comes out of your faucet is safe to drink. It might taste funny, though, because of germ-killing chemicals added during sewage treatment.

**Yikes!** It wasn't until the 1800s that flush toilets and sewer systems became common as a way to control human waste. Before that time, people had to use outhouses. An outhouse was a small building away from the main house that had a hole in the ground for pooping and peeing. People also used chamber pots inside their home. They would do their business in this pot and once it got filled up with waste, they would empty it outside.

Rainwater that drains off city streets and country fields is not usually treated before it flows into rivers and streams. During big storms, sewer systems may overflow. Then raw sewage from homes and businesses mixes with rainwater and gets into streams and rivers, and sometimes into people's basements.

In some communities, sewer pipes are old and cracked. Untreated sewage may leak out, polluting streams and lakes. Then bacteria, viruses, parasites, and poisonous chemicals may get into drinking and swimming water. According to the U.S. Environmental Protection Agency, the amount of untreated sewage that pollutes the environment in each county every year would be enough to fill the Empire State Building and Madison Square Garden!

Can you tell if water is clean by the way it looks? Not always. Say you go hiking in the woods and you come to a creek. You are really thirsty, and that flowing water looks so clean and refreshing. You would just love a sip. But do you know what's in that water? There's a good chance that deer, bears, and other forest animals may have been peeing and pooping in or near the

**Yikes!** Some farmers use animal poop as fertilizer to help their crops grow. Flooding rains can carry this poop into creeks, streams, rivers, and lakes. So people can wind up drinking germs and chemicals from animal poop!

water before it reached you. Fish and other water animals add their own wastes, too. (If you have ever kept fish in a tank, you know how much fish can poop!) Poop has a lot of germs. So drinking this kind of water could make you sick.

Sometimes swimming places, such as the ocean or reservoirs, can get pretty yucky as well. A poopy diaper on a toddler playing in a reservoir can spread germs through the water. A swimmer who swallows a mouthful of germ-filled water may soon wind up with diarrhea. You should be careful swimming in ponds, as well. These are popular hangouts for geese—and geese leave behind *a lot* of poop!

CHAPTER
THREE

# Trashed

## LITTER BUG

How would you feel if empty bottles, soda cans, pieces of paper, and other bits of garbage littered the ground all over your neighborhood? Litter can make a beautiful landscape look really ugly. More importantly, litter is a form of pollution.

What happens to litter? If someone doesn't pick it up, is it stuck in the ground forever? That depends. Certain kinds of household trash, such as a banana peel or an apple core, can decompose (break down into pieces or rot). Sunlight, rain, bacteria, insects, and worms all work to turn this kind of trash into a grayish, yucky mess. After just a few days or weeks outside, you couldn't even tell what they had been. Eventually, these items will become a part of the soil.

Some types of trash take a lot longer to decompose, though. And glass and many plastic items cannot decompose at all. So they could end up stuck in the ground forever!

Litter is harmful to the environment—and makes places like this river look yucky, too!

**Yikes!** A paper bag left outside will rot away within a month, but a plastic bag may take 15 to 1,000 years to decompose! A cigarette butt may hang around for two to five years, an aluminum can for 80 to 100 years, and a disposable diaper may take 500 to 800 years to decompose. A Styrofoam cup or a glass bottle may last forever!

# GARBAGE DUMPS

What kinds of things have you tossed in the trash can today? An empty juice carton? A napkin? Part of a sandwich left over from lunch? The average American throws away more than four pounds (1.8 kg) of garbage each day. Considering there are more than 300 million people in the United States, that's a lot of garbage! So what do the garbage trucks do with all that garbage they collect every week?

For many years, people's trash was hauled off to open garbage dumps. The dump was basically a hole in the ground where people tossed all kinds of waste. But the rotting garbage attracted a lot of unwanted guests. Soon the dumps were overrun with disease-carrying pests, such as flies, mosquitoes, and rats. Rainwater washed dirt and sometimes poisonous chemicals from the dump into nearby streams. Eventually this yucky stuff ended up in the water supply people used to drink and bathe.

**Yikes!** During ancient times, people threw their garbage right out their back doors. As it piled up outside, the rotting garbage smelled awful! By the 1700s, cities started collecting trash to get it off the streets and away from waterways.

The open dumps were unbelievably stinky, dirty, and dangerous. Eventually, they were closed down and replaced with a safer way to get rid of trash. These days, most garbage is hauled away to landfills. In a landfill, garbage is still buried, but it does not harm the environment. The bottom of a landfill is lined with layers of clay or plastic to keep liquid waste from spilling into the soil. Workers spread fresh soil over the garbage pile each day.

This landfill is lined with layers of plastic to keep harmful pollutants from the garbage out of the nearby soil.

Once a landfill is full, it is sealed and covered with clay and dirt. Unlike open garbage dumps, most of the garbage in landfills does not decompose. It can stay there for a *very* long time.

**Garbage is buried in a landfill.**

CHAPTER
FOUR

# Pollution at Home

## INVISIBLE DANGERS

Have you ever been in a room that had just been painted? It was probably so smelly that you had to leave the room. Many paints and varnishes contain chemicals that are sent into the air in the form of invisible gas or fumes. They may get into your body when you breathe. After a while, you may feel dizzy, get a headache, or feel sick to your stomach.

Many household products, such as ammonia, bleach, and other cleaners, also contain chemicals that can make you sick when you inhale them. The chemicals in bleach, for example, are so strong that inhaling them for just a short time can damage the

inside of your nose and throat. The fumes may also make your eyes red and watery.

If you live in an old house, it may have some pollutants your family doesn't even know about. Until the mid-1970s, for example, asbestos was commonly used as a building material. Asbestos

is fireproof and was placed between walls to
help keep buildings safe from fire. But scientists
now know that it can cause cancer. Years ago,
workers using this material often breathed in large
amounts of asbestos fibers, which entered their
lungs. Many of these workers later developed lung
cancer.

Asbestos is no longer used in the United
States, but many homes still contain this material.
People who live in buildings that have asbestos are
not in danger—as long as they leave the material
alone. But if they cut through a wall or roof
containing asbestos, they will shake some of the
fibers loose. Then the fibers will float through the
air and can be breathed in.

# THANKS FOR NOT SMOKING

If you have a family member who smokes, you're
probably used to living in a smoke-filled house.
But cigarette smoking is a major cause of indoor
air pollution. Cigarettes contain about 4,000
chemicals. At least 200 of them are poisonous.
These poisons can damage the lungs and cause

Cigarette smoke contains chemicals that can be harmful to your health—whether you are the smoker or not. The top photo shows part of the lung of a long-time smoker. (Healthy lungs are all pink.)

serious breathing problems. In addition, many poisons in cigarette smoke can cause cancer of the mouth, throat, and lungs, which may develop after years of cigarette smoking.

When a smoker takes a puff and then breathes out, chemicals in the smoke are sent out into the air. Everyone around the smoker breathes in these chemicals, too. If you don't smoke, but spend time near someone who does, you are breathing in secondhand smoke. Inhaling somebody else's smoke can give you the same kinds of health problems that smokers develop. Secondhand smoke can also trigger asthma attacks or make asthma symptoms worse.

**Yikes!** Kids who live with someone who smokes get sick more often than those whose homes are free of secondhand smoke.

# GET THE LEAD OUT

If you live in an old home, another kind of yucky pollution may be hiding out there. It's lead. Lead is a metal used in batteries, shotgun pellets, and building materials. It used to be commonly found in paint.

If lead gets into the body, though, it can cause a lot of trouble. Lead can build up in the body. It can poison the brain and nerves, the muscles, and other body systems.

Water pipes used to be made of lead. Many old buildings still have these lead pipes. When water flows through lead pipes, tiny amounts of lead pass into it. Hot water carries more lead out of pipes than cold water. Today, builders use mostly copper and plastic for pipes, but the glue that holds the joints of copper pipes together contains lead.

Until 1978, paints containing lead were still used on buildings, furniture, and toys. Some of these items are still around. Like asbestos, lead paint is not dangerous unless it is damaged. But old paint may crack and peel. Young children sometimes like to put things into their mouths.

# A History Lesson

During the first few centuries AD, the Roman Empire included much of Europe and parts of Asia and Africa. But the Empire eventually broke apart. Some scientists say that lead poisoning may have been to blame.

The ancient Romans painted their walls with lead paint, used lead pipes for their water, and flavored their wine with grape syrup made in lead pots. Some of the Roman emperors suffered from symptoms of lead poisoning. According to one Canadian scientist, a single teaspoon of the grape syrup would be enough to cause lead poisoning.

If they chew on a peeled-off paint chip or an old painted toy, they will swallow bits of lead. Other family members may take in lead, too, if bits of it mix in with dust that gets into the air they breathe.

In the United States, there are now laws against using lead in paint, water pipes, and other products.

# Our Gassy World

## CLIMATE CHANGE

All over the world, people depend on fuel to run their cars, heat their homes and office buildings, and power their computers. But burning fuel produces lots of chemicals that are polluting our air, water, and soil. One of these products is a gas called carbon dioxide. Every year, people's activities pour billions of tons of carbon dioxide into the atmosphere.

Scientists call carbon dioxide a greenhouse gas. Carbon dioxide and certain other gases in the atmosphere act like the windows of a greenhouse. They trap heat close to Earth's surface. Scientists say that these greenhouse

Factories like this oil refinery burn lots of fuel and release greenhouse gases into the environment.

gases are adding to the warming of our planet. This temperature rise could bring major changes in our environment, our lives, and the lives of all Earth's creatures.

These days, many people talk a lot about "going green"—that is, conserving energy and reducing pollution to help the environment. Climate change is not something that *might* happen in the future. It is happening right now, and we are already seeing the effects. In general, summers are getting hotter, and winters are getting milder. But these signs are only the start. The warming trend is expected to speed up and produce even greater effects. Large areas at the North and South poles are covered with ice. But that ice is starting to melt. This has led to rising sea levels. If sea levels rise too much, eventually they could flood coastal cities all over the world.

Climate change may already be affecting the weather in various parts of the planet. Earth is having more storms with violent winds and flooding. Wildlife species could be forced to either adapt, move, or become extinct as their habitats change.

Cows, goats, buffalo, camels, and sheep burp out methane, a powerful greenhouse gas that is contributing to climate change.

# WHO'S PASSING GAS?

Would you believe that cow farts are actually adding to the warming of our planet? Bacteria that live in the guts of cows help to digest their food. These bacteria turn some of the food into methane gas. So every time a cow burps or

## Burpless Cows

Researchers in Australia and New Zealand are working to develop "burpless" grass for cattle. They are trying to make the grass more digestible so that the cows that eat it won't have to chew and burp as much. This would help cut down the amount of air-polluting methane they produce.

"passes gas," it releases methane into the air. Sheep, goats, buffalo, and camels burp out methane, too. Methane is a powerful greenhouse gas. In fact, it traps twenty-five times more heat than carbon dioxide. Everybody knows that farts are yucky, but who knew they could cause pollution, too?

As human populations continue to grow, so does the demand for meat and dairy products. The number of cattle has doubled since the 1950s. More cattle means more farts.

❋ ❋ ❋ ❋

These days, most people don't think it's polite to spit on the floor or throw dishwater out the window. But they may still drop cigarette butts on the ground or throw a paper cup or burger wrapper out the car window. And all too often they see the ocean as a convenient place to dump garbage and other wastes. We've come a long way, but we still have a lot of work to do to battle the yucky pollution in our world.

# WORDS TO KNOW

**bacteria** Microscopic single-celled organisms. Some cause diseases. Others are involved in rotting.

**decompose** To break down into pieces; to rot.

**fertilizer** A substance added to the soil to help crops grow.

**greenhouse gas** A heat-trapping gas involved in global climate change.

**landfill** A low area containing buried waste material.

**pollutant** A substance that makes air, soil, or water dirty or harmful to living things.

**scum** A yucky layer of material that floats to the top of dirty water when it is allowed to stand for a while.

**secondhand smoke** Tobacco smoke that is inhaled by a nonsmoker.

**sludge** A yucky layer of material that sinks to the bottom of dirty water when it is allowed to stand for a while.

**smog** A mixture of fog and smoke that can be irritating or even deadly.

# FURTHER READING

Cherry, Lynne, and Gary Braasch. *How We Know What We Know About Our Changing Climate: Scientists and Kids Explore Global Warming*. Nevada City, Calif.: Dawn Publications, 2008.

Green, Jen. *Reducing Air Pollution*. Strongsville, Ohio: Gareth Stevens, 2005.

Orme, Helen. *Pollution*. New York: Bearport Publishing, 2008.

Price, Sean. *Water Pollution*. Tarrytown, N.Y.: Marshall Cavendish Children's Books, 2008.

Rapp, Valerie. *Protecting Earth's Air Quality*. Minneapolis, Minn.: Lerner Publishing Group, 2008.

Wilcox, Charlotte. *Earth-Friendly Waste Management*. Minneapolis, Minn.: Lerner Publishing Group, 2009.

# INTERNET ADDRESSES

Environmental Protection Agency. "Environmental Kids
   Club." 2009.
   <http://www.epa.gov/kids/>

OneWorld UK. "Pollution: Muck, Stink, and Poison."
   <http://tiki.oneworld.net/pollution/pollution_home.
   html>

Sacramento Metropolitan Air Quality Management
   District (SMAQMD). "Smog City." 1999.
   <http://smogcity.com/>

# Index